AF

For
Brian McMaster
and
The Welsh National Opera

JULIAN MITCHELL

AFTER AIDA
or
Verdi's Messiah

 Please return to
the
Maddermarket
Theatre

AMBER LANE PRESS

All rights whatsoever in this play are strictly reserved and
application for permission to perform the play, etc. must be made
in advance, before rehearsals begin, to: A. D. Peters & Co. Ltd. of
10 Buckingham Street, London WC2N 6BU.

No performance may be given unless a licence has been obtained.

First published in 1986 by
Amber Lane Press Ltd
9 Middle Way
Oxford OX2 7LH

Printed in Great Britain by
Cotswold Press Ltd., Oxford

ISBN: 0 906399 68 8

CONDITIONS OF SALE

INTRODUCTION

The Welsh passion for choral singing has been noted for at least eight hundred years. Giraldus Cambrensis, himself half-Welsh, observed in 1188 that in Wales even small children sang in parts. So too did tiny babies, the moment they stopped screaming. That passion is still very much alive today, and it was local choirs which provided the basis for the Welsh National Opera when it began in 1946. For many years the chorus continued to be voluntary, though it is fully professional now, and shares the company's international reputation for the highest standards of operatic singing, playing and production.

All WNO's work originates in Wales. Its headquarters, offices, workshops and rehearsal rooms are all in Cardiff. But the company is obliged to give more performances outside Wales than in, because only Cardiff, Swansea and Llandudno have theatres large enough for grand opera. Yet anyone who dared to suggest that love of opera was confined to the hinterland of those places would immediately set a furious chorus buzzing (in parts) round his ears. To overcome the problem, the WNO has developed a series of 'small tours' to take some sort of opera to the farthest corners of Wales. It was for just such a 'small tour' that Brian McMaster, the Managing Director, chief magician and Machiavelli of the company, asked me to write a play about opera. And on a small tour *Verdi's Messiah,* as *After Aida* was first known, went. It opened in Swansea — not at the Grand Theatre, but at the much smaller Taliesin. It went on to other small theatres in Mold, Harlech, Lampeter and Milford Haven, to town halls (Brecon, Maesteg, Pontypridd), school halls (Llangollen, Cardigan), a cinema in an Arts Centre at Builth Wells and a community centre in Llanidloes. Since these venues couldn't possibly accommodate both orchestra and audience, the singers were accompanied only by a piano. The set and the lighting changed from one auditorium to another. Nonetheless a play about Verdi and his librettist Boito, combining singers and actors, did cover the principality.

I didn't set out to write about Verdi and Boito — indeed I knew almost nothing about them when Brian approached me: I knew, in fact, very little about opera. When I lived in London I'd been put off it by the appallingly pretentious audience and the generally

vile standard of productions, received with largely bogus
applause. Though I have always loved listening to singing, I
thought opera as an art form was dead, and preferred to listen to
records at home rather than cover my eyes in the gaudy mauso-
leums where ludicrously amateur acting went on in front of vast
swags of pompous set. Why pay huge sums of money to sit with
one's eyes shut? London theatre offered far more lively entertain-
ment.

But when I came to live in South Wales, where theatrical vitality
is relatively low, I started going to WNO productions. Quite soon I
was a subscriber. Though the New Theatre, Cardiff, is hardly ideal
for opera, it is quite intimate: opera doesn't come at you across
acres of baldness and tiaras. The WNO even made the libretti of
operas available before productions, so one could actually know
what was going on. The singing was excellent, and so was the
orchestra; but what really hooked me were the productions. The
WNO used producers who tried to make opera alive and relevant.
And the audience was so much more genuine than in London. On
the first night of the season, both Welsh and English national
anthems were played. I shall never forget a splendid mezzo
soaring out from the upper circle in 'Hen wlad fy nhadau'. This
wasn't opera for an elite, it was opera for people who loved
singing.

Not that WNO converted me to *all* opera. I remain highly scep-
tical about Wagner: anyone who takes that long to speak his mind
may well not have as much to say as he thinks. And the lack of
dramatic action in Handel makes me extremely fidgety. But I have
learned that there is much more to Bellini than fancy roulades,
and that Puccini can actually be as good as one thought at seven-
teen. (The WNO *Madame Butterfly* is the single best opera production I have so far seen: unless that's Janacek's *From the House of the
Dead* — Janacek has been a special WNO revelation.) But above all I
have come to realise that Verdi is as great a genius as Shakespeare
— the writer he himself admired above all others except Dante.

Brian McMaster's original idea was that I should write something about the backstage life of an opera company, showing all
the secret drama that goes on before an opera is presented to the
public. So I took singing lessons to try and feel what it might be
like to be a real singer, and I attended rehearsals of operas and
music calls of individual singers, and talked to everyone I could —

directors (called producers in the opera), conductors, repetiteurs, designers, singers. But the more I discovered, the less I felt I knew. Opera is astonishingly different from theatre in almost every way. I'd imagined, for instance, that singers operated more or less like actors. But they have an entirely different training, which leads to a wholly separate approach. Partly this is tradition; partly it's the sheer physical difficulty of singing. A singer will spend months learning and characterising a part with a musical coach from the company, and perhaps a private teacher as well. He will arrive at the first rehearsal having studied the role minutely, treating the composer's lightest indication with the utmost respect. The music on the page is sacred. An actor, in contrast, learns his lines and develops his character during the process of rehearsal. The text (at least of a new play) is subject to alteration and rewriting right up to the first night — and often after it. Singers, like trams, keep to the musical tracks. Actors, like dodgem-cars, are free to drive at any speed and in any direction, under the director's supervision, within the confines of the play. As a result the philosophies of the performers are completely different, and frequently at odds. I have yet to meet a singer who thinks it worth his or her while to take acting lessons, for instance. But almost every actor I know has taken singing lessons.

The dominance of the music in opera means that responsibility for characterisation really lies with the conductor. He controls the tempo, the volume, the emphasis. Perhaps this explains why there are so many 'controversial' opera productions: the producer has relatively little to do, compared to a theatre director, and has time to devote to reinterpretation and visual hi-jinks. But there is still a dangerous no-man's land, frequently disputed, between conductor and producer, an area full of sudden explosions and snapped batons where opera and theatre clash. Ultimately, strength of personality prevails; each combination comes up with its own compromise.

So much of this was mysterious to me that I began to feel I would never be able to write about opera. Then Richard Armstrong, WNO's musical director, under the flattering illusion that I was already familiar with the lives of the great composers, suggested I look at a new collection of anecdotes about Verdi. In my ignorance they made little sense to me, but they did make me want to know more about Verdi. So I read the biographies, and in Frank

Walker's *The Man Verdi* found my subject in a long chapter about
Verdi and Boito. Here was something I felt I did understand — a
great artist going through a crisis, brought back to composition
after a long silence, and finding himself a substitute prodigal son
in the process. I read the Verdi/Boito correspondence, Julian
Budden's invaluable volumes on the operas, one or two minor
sources — then settled to the most enjoyable 'research' I've ever
done. Day after day I had a perfect excuse to play through Verdi's
operas to find suitable pieces for my play. (It was always understood that it was to include operatic extracts.)

I begin with the end of *Aida*, because it seemed, for ten years and
more, to be the end of Verdi's career, and could well have been
taken as his farewell to music. The *Rigoletto* quartet follows
because it is one of the two pieces he composed himself at which
Verdi is known to have wept — the other being the overture to the
third act of *La Traviata*, which would never have had the same
impact on a piano. I wanted to show that Verdi had a very good
idea of the value of his own work, and excellent reason to despise
his critics. The 'Lux aeterna' from the *Requiem* was the natural
counterblast to Boito's *Mephistopheles:* Christian light against the
prince of darkness. The end of Act II of *Ernani* seemed to mirror
what Boito must have felt as he found himself handing his outline
of *Otello* to Verdi. The Sleepwalking Scene from *Macbeth* not only
shows how advanced Verdi already was, thirty years before *Otello*,
but how Shakespeare had already once inspired him to extra-
ordinary music. The aria from *Simon Boccanegra* is there to show
how Boito, for all his admiration for 'the music of the future',
could still appreciate a wonderful 'number'. The debate about
music theatre which runs throughout the play comes to its climax,
I hope, in the extracts I've chosen from *Otello* itself. In arranging
and in some cases considerably adapting this music, Martin
André sometimes found himself in that no-man's land I've mentioned. Was this a play with music, a play illustrating music; was it
theatre or opera, or both? If it's all of these things, as I would like it
to be, then the hybrid owes him a very great deal and I am truly
grateful.

While I was writing the play the limitations imposed by a 'small
tour' — one set, as few actors and singers as possible — soon came
to feel a positive liberation. I grew up with the 'well-made' play,
now creaking and groaning its last, and believe that playwrights

have only just begun to rediscover the freedom of drama to make anything and everything happen on a single stage. But it was only with Howard Davies's ideas for the production that I realised just how free one can be. Having cast the play with wonderful actors, Howard conceived the production as a rehearsal for the first night of *Otello*, taking place in a disused theatre (as rehearsals so often do). Bob Crowley's design was brilliant — tiers of tired plush seats, crying out, like Verdi himself, to be restored to their true purpose. Howard kept all the actors and singers on stage throughout, so there was no need for conventional entrances and exits. The story flowed directly from one scene to the next, and the singing was wholly integrated with the play. In fact he made more of *Verdi's Messiah* than I had dared to think possible. From now on I shall assume that's what directors are for.

The play shows how one particular work of art came to be made. I hope it may persuade some people, who feel as I used to feel myself, that opera is dead, that it is nothing of the sort, that it is simply waiting to be restored to its role as a truly popular art — which it was in Verdi's and Boito's day.

Julian Mitchell, Llanvaches, Gwent, 1985

After Aida was commissioned by the Welsh National Opera, and first performed under the title *Verdi's Messiah* at the Taliesin Theatre, Swansea on October 24th, 1985. It was directed by Howard Davies with the following cast:

VERDI:	Richard Griffiths
STREPPONI:	Zoë Wanamaker
RICORDI:	Malcolm Storry
FACCIO:	David Lyon
BOITO:	Ian Charleson
SOPRANO:	Christine Teare
MEZZO-SOPRANO:	Wendy Verco
TENOR:	Michael Burch
BASS/BARITONE:	Jonathan Best

Musical Director and Pianist: Martin André

Designer: Bob Crowley
Lighting: Michael Spray
Assistant to the Designer: Rod Langsford
Company and Stage Manager: Ruth Sallis

After Aida was first presented in London, at the Old Vic, on March 19th, 1986, with following changes of cast:

STREPPONI:	Gemma Jones
SOPRANO:	Elizabeth Collier/ Christine Teare
MEZZO-SOPRANO:	Beverly Mills/ Wendy Verco
TENOR:	Mark Hamilton/ John Harris
BASS/BARITONE:	Henry Newman/ Steven Page

AFTER AIDA

CHARACTERS

GIUSEPPE VERDI
ARRIGO BOITO
GIUSEPPINA STREPPONI, Verdi's wife
GIULIO RICORDI
FRANCO FACCIO

SOPRANO
MEZZO-SOPRANO
TENOR
BASS/BARITONE

PIANIST

CHARACTERS

ACT ONE

The stage is dark. Then a very dim light reveals AIDA *and* RADAMES *in one another's arms in the pyramid tomb from the end of 'Aida'. They are joined by* AMNERIS *and sing 'O world farewell'. As they finish a light comes up on a figure sitting with folded arms. It is* GIUSEPPE VERDI, *a neat, trim man of 66, with a white beard and a glaring eye.*

VERDI: I don't compose. Not any longer.
[*He rises.*]
Do you know what some damned fool critic said about *Aida*? He said, 'Verdi doesn't know how to write for singers'! Tone-deaf! The man's tone-deaf! [*mimicking a high-falutin' critic*] 'What little good there is in Verdi's music is derived entirely from Gounod, Meyerbeer and Wagner' — *Wagner*, of course. So now you know.
[*Pause.*]
I've done my best, people have cheered and booed — It's been a good life. No complaints. But it's over. Here lies Giuseppe Verdi, the imitation Wagner, thank you and good night.
[*He becomes all sweet reason.*]
It's better I *don't* compose. The public's had forty years of me and my trash, it's been very patient, but enough's enough. I've done. [*sly grin*] That bloody critic wrote for my photograph once. Well, I'm always *delighted* to give my portrait to my friends. But my enemies — they can damn well go and buy it. Critics! We did *Aida* in Parma once. First-class production, though I say so myself. Good scenery, good orchestra, *very* good chorus, excellent principals. For once in my life a genuine artistic success. And what happens? Some snivelling ignoramus from Reggio Emilia decides to jump on the train and come and have a look. Doesn't like it. Very inferior stuff, he *opines*. Such mediocre twaddle, in fact, I ought to refund him the price of his ticket, his train-fare *and* his supper. Give him the ticket and train-fare, I said, but

bugger his supper. He should have eaten before he set out. [*harsh laugh*] Then I published our correspondence in the papers. [*sings*] 'O critic, farewell!' [*smile*] I'm a bear, of course. People have always said so. Doesn't know how to behave — a peasant is always a peasant — can't say the right thing ever. [*parody*] My dear, what a talent! Such expressiveness! It couldn't *be* sung better! The voice is *divine*! There's been nothing like it for fifty years — a hundred — a thousand! And the chorus! And the orchestra! And the barmen and the cloakroom attendants and the — The opera? Oh, I don't know. Some rubbish of Verdi's, I believe. One doesn't go to the opera for the *opera*, for heaven's sake! But wherever you go, it's the world's leading theatre, no doubt about it. [*angry*] La Scala, San Carlo, La Fenice — St Petersburg, Vienna, Paris — it's always the finest theatre in the world. In Paris, it's the finest theatre in two or three worlds. And I'm just an ignorant country bumpkin who thinks one decent second-class theatre might be a damned sight better than all these leading ones. Because I *am* a peasant, I was born a peasant, I've been an ordinary workhand, a day-labourer, bringing my goods to be exploited by the publishers. Oh, yes, my publishers, the Ricordis, they exploited me. *Defrauded* me. For years. Till I caught on. Then I made them send me all the contracts from *Rigoletto* on. Twenty years of contracts. I went through them line by line. Twenty years of swindling. They coughed up something in the end — not nearly enough. But I do business with the grandson now. Giulio Ricordi, clever young man. Started with a lot of tomfool ideas about 'the music of the future', but he's grown up. Grown up a lot. He's even more or less honest. Well, if anyone is.

[*Cynicism is mixed with incredulity.*]

Can you imagine? Starting to cheat with *Rigoletto*! Ricordi starting to cheat with *Rigoletto*!

[*Pause, then he smiles.*]

Of course, that's an opera that proves once and for

all that Verdi can't write for singers. It reeks of Gounod and Wagner. It's hopelessly un-Italian, unmelodious, unharmonic, undramatic! The quartet's a complete shambles. Rigoletto and Gilda one side of the stage watching the Duke wooing Magdalena on the other. One man mad for vengeance, the other for women, one girl broken-hearted, the other no better than she should be. It's pure trash, the whole thing.

[*The* SINGERS *sing the quartet from 'Rigoletto'.* VERDI *listens with great intensity. By the end he is in tears.*]

That's why I don't compose. I can't write for singers.

[*We now discover* GIULIO RICORDI, GIUSEPPINA STREPPONI *and* FRANCO FACCIO. STREPPONI *is 64 now, and long retired from the stage on which she was once a successful soprano. She has been with* VERDI, *first as his mistress, then as his wife, for 32 years, and things have not been at all easy for the last decade —* VERDI *having fallen in love with another singer. The worst is now over, however, and she has settled into the role of secretary and guard-dog, the person through whom everyone has to go to reach* VERDI. GIULIO RICORDI *is 39, small, trim, spare, with a very quick and lively mind. He is the third* RICORDI *in the family publishing business.* FACCIO *is 39, too, an old friend of* RICORDI's, *and* VERDI's *most trusted younger conductor.*]

STREPPONI: Oh, well, if he'd listen to me! But he doesn't, Giulio. I have no influence at all. He does precisely what he wants. And what he wants is to farm.

RICORDI: I don't believe it. His whole life has been opera. Except the *Requiem*, of course.

FACCIO: Even the *Requiem* is opera of a sort.

STREPPONI: Franco —

FACCIO: As a matter of fact, it's the most operatic Requiem ever written.

STREPPONI: Verdi may not be a formal Christian, but the feeling is there in the music.

FACCIO: Oh, of course. But the individual sections are just

	like operatic numbers — arias, duets, trios, quartets. And when we perform it in theatres —
STREPPONI:	Perhaps you shouldn't.
RICORDI:	Of course they should! It's a great *religious opera*. In fact, I should like to see it done outdoors. In the streets.
STREPPONI:	Giulio!
RICORDI:	Verdi's music has always belonged to the people. Italian patriots sang his tunes as they fought for their freedom. His name *meant* Italy. If the *Requiem* was sung in the great squares of our cities, people would fall to their knees and weep for what they've lost — the greatest composer Italy ever produced, nine years without an opera! When Italian music is threatened by French and German — nine years of silence! It's high treason!
STREPPONI:	You wouldn't dare say that to his face.
RICORDI:	No, but —
STREPPONI:	Then don't expect me to.
RICORDI:	Signora, we have *got* to get him back to work.
STREPPONI:	He *is* working. On the farm.
FACCIO:	But is he happy?
STREPPONI:	Oh, well — happy!
RICORDI:	It's so perverse!
STREPPONI:	No. He feels his kind of music is no longer what the public wants.
RICORDI:	But they do want it!
STREPPONI:	No. They want Wagner.
RICORDI:	They want Wagner *and* Verdi.
STREPPONI:	Some people thought *Aida* was old-fashioned. They said so.
FACCIO:	Some people simply can't hear.
STREPPONI:	But it wasn't Wagnerian. And he can't and won't write Wagnerian music.
FACCIO:	There's some awfully good Wagner, actually.
STREPPONI:	Of course. Verdi admires him very much. But he thinks his influence is very harmful to Italian composers. He thinks Italians should write Italian music, not German.
RICORDI:	Well, so do I. So long as they *write*.
STREPPONI:	The critics don't. The critics think Wagner is

everything new and wonderful, while Verdi — Giulio, he's afraid he wouldn't even get a fair hearing now.

RICORDI: I guarantee him a triumph — if only he'll *write*.

STREPPONI: He won't.

FACCIO: What about a singer? Couldn't he be tempted to write *for* someone? Patti, for instance? He admires Adelina Patti.

RICORDI: I've tried that.

FACCIO: Oh.

RICORDI: A subject — that's what he needs. Something to fire his imagination.

FACCIO: Or someone. A writer he really admires. Hugo, for instance. He's always been fond of Victor Hugo.

RICORDI: Old-fashioned. And all the good plots done.

FACCIO: Shakespeare? He's only ever done one Shakespeare.

STREPPONI: He likes *Lear*. He keeps a version by his bed.

FACCIO: There we are then!

STREPPONI: Unfortunately he's kept it there for thirty years.

FACCIO: What about *Cleopatra*? Didn't he talk about doing *Cleopatra* once?

RICORDI: No suitable singer.

STREPPONI: Cleopatra has to be — trim.

FACCIO: And he's done *Macbeth*.

RICORDI: And you've done *Hamlet*.

FACCIO: Please!

RICORDI: It wasn't bad. Not nearly as bad as Mercadante's. Or Buzzolla's. Or Zanardini's. Or Moroni's, come to that.

FACCIO: Shall we just say that *Hamlet's* been done to death and leave it at that?

RICORDI: Of course, you had the advantage of a very good libretto.

FACCIO: Very.

STREPPONI: Oh, don't let's go through all that again, please!

RICORDI: Arrigo Boito *is* the best librettist in Italy.

STREPPONI: He's also out of the question.

[*Pause.*]

RICORDI: Of course, you know what hasn't been done.

STREPPONI: *Henry the Sixth Part Three*?

RICORDI: *Othello.*

STREPPONI: What about the Rossini version?

RICORDI: No resemblance to Shakespeare.

FACCIO: Wonderful characters. Othello — Desdemona —
              Iago. Actually, I've never really understood Iago.

RICORDI: You should be a publisher. There's plenty of
              motiveless malignancy in the music business,
              believe me.

STREPPONI: It is a good subject. Very good. But who could we
              get to do the libretto?
              [*Pause.*]

RICORDI: You know what I think.

FACCIO: I agree with Giulio.

STREPPONI: Verdi wouldn't even consider him.

RICORDI: Boito is a poet, you know. Quite a remarkable poet.

FACCIO: And a composer.

STREPPONI: *Mephistopheles*! You call that an opera!

FACCIO: He played me a bit of his new opera the other day.
              It's very — very original.

STREPPONI: What's it about? The devil himself this time?

FACCIO: No. Well — the Emperor Nero.

STREPPONI: [*laughs*] I don't know why you keep suggesting him.
              He's the opposite of Verdi in every way.

RICORDI: Opposites often make excellent collaborators.

STREPPONI: But Verdi hates that sort of smart Bohemian.

FACCIO: Oh, he is odd, of course — well, eccentric. But he's
              a good chap really. And Verdi's forgiven me for
              being young once. He's forgiven Giulio for enthu-
              sing over Wagner. Why can't he forgive Boito?

STREPPONI: He never forgives an insult.

FACCIO: It wasn't meant as an insult.

RICORDI: And Boito has made the most handsome amends.
              He even offered Verdi the libretto of *Nero*.

STREPPONI: Oh, very kind!

RICORDI: And Verdi was very impressed with what he did
              with *Hamlet* for Franco.

FACCIO: Yes, well — it was so much better than the music.

RICORDI: The point is, signora, he's the only man who truly
              understands what a composer wants and needs.

STREPPONI: Well, I'm not going to suggest him. [*to* FACCIO]
              And if I were you, I wouldn't mention him either.

Verdi might well refuse to let you conduct his work.
again ever.

FACCIO: Up to you, then, Giulio!

RICORDI: It would come much better from you, signora.
Verdi knows we're both Arrigo's friend.

STREPPONI: Arrigo! Arrigo Boito! Even his name's ridiculous!

[ARRIGO BOITO *is discovered — a dandyish figure,*
tall and fair, 37, with a pince-nez. He bursts into 'La
donna è mobile'. When he reaches the piano he breaks
off to take a glass of wine from the piano-lid, where a
bottle and glasses are standing. He addresses the
audience.]

BOITO: *Rigoletto* is, of course, a very great work of art, by a
composer of unquestioned genius, and no one
admires art and genius more than myself. *However*
— it does happen to contain the single most irrita-
tingly catchy tune in the entire history of opera, a
fact immediately exploited with malicious acuity
by every pseudo-intellectual organ-grinder in Italy
within five minutes of the first-night curtain,
which, for those of you with a taste for music-
ological pedantry, was precisely 11.47 on March
11th 1851, at the Teatro La Fenice, Venice, into
whose noxious night-stale, locally known as
lagoons, I should personally have been only too
happy to let the mobile madonna sink without
murmur. Not that it's not a good aria. It's fantast-
ically good, damn it. But it buzzes for weeks in
your head, like a wasp in an attic. It deafens you to
everything else, like a twenty-one-gun salute.
[*confidentially*] By the way, about the curtain coming
down at 11.47, I made that up. But it fooled you,
didn't it? You must sound authoritative when
you're sounding off. I discovered that when I was a
critic. You can talk absolute rubbish, but if you
sound all right, people will swallow every word.
[*sings unaccompanied*] 'La donna è mobile, qual
piuma al vento —' God, what a tune! I can't write
tunes. [*gloom*] I can't write anything. I've had it.
Poor old Arrigo! [*cheering up*] I wasn't christened
Arrigo. I was christened Enrico. Very plebeian. I

changed that as soon as I could. But my mother —
she was Polish. A countess. Have you ever heard of
a Polish woman who wasn't a countess? My mother
liked me to play and sing. So —
> [*He barges the* PIANIST *off his stool.*]

Move over, maestro. An infant prodigy is about to
perform for his Polish Mamma. [*mimicking his
mother's Polish voice*] Enrico, darling, play for your
Polish Mamma, play 'La donna è mobile', please,
darling, sing to me, I am so sad.
> [*He begins to play very plonkingly, singing
> 'Waa–waa–waa–waa–waa–waa', then breaking off
> and beating his fists against the piano.*]

I can't, I can't, I can't! Not again! [*Polish mother*]
Enrico, Enrico darling! Play for me, please! Play 'La
donna è mobile', you know how I love it. [*child*]
Won't! Shan't! [*bangs his head on the keys*] Hate you!
[*Polish mother, unimpressed*] Darling, your temper-
ment, you get it from me! [*adult, to the audience*]
Useless, whatever I did. Weeping, wailing,
whining — 'La donna è mobile'! So what could I do
to escape her? I could improvise, that's what I
could do. The little prodigy, half-Polish, half-
Italian, could turn that magnificent Italian buzz-
saw into — [*turns it into a polka*] — a thoroughly
Polish polka! [*leaps up, applauding himself*] Bravo!
Bravo!
> [FACCIO *has come to listen with the* PIANIST.]

FACCIO: I hope Verdi doesn't know *that*.

BOITO: Oh, he knows everything. He even knows how to
write music!

FACCIO: Might there be a glass of that for me?

BOITO: Help yourself. Fill mine while you're at it.

FACCIO: Thanks.
> [*He fills the glasses.*]

BOITO: Of course, the trouble with Verdi is, he's a great
artist who's never given a toss for the principles of
art.

FACCIO: And the trouble with you is, you spend so much
time on the principles, you've no energy left for the
art.

BOITO: I can't write music unless I know what I'm doing.
Theoretically, I mean. No one can. Except you
damned Italians. You just sit down and *emote*.
That's why there's so much crap about.

FACCIO: Well, show us what thinking can do. Get on with
Nero.

BOITO: I can't. I don't know what I'm doing. Oh, I know
what I'm *doing*. I'm writing a grand opera about the
fundamental conflict between good and evil in the
universe.

FACCIO: Oh, good. I always enjoy a comedy.

BOITO: The only comic thing about it is, I can't do it. All I
can do is rehash other men's plays and squeeze
them down into libretti for unthinking, sponta-
neous, illiterate — or at least alogic, shall we say —

FACCIO: Don't you mean analphabetic?

BOITO: — *emotional* composers to drown my painfully
chosen words in sticky, catchy, unforgettable *tunes*.

FACCIO: You do do it awfully well, though.

BOITO: But I wanted not to be like my father!

FACCIO: What *do* you mean?

BOITO: He painted miniatures, Franco. Very tiny pictures.
Of very minor nobility. And he painted them very,
very badly.

FACCIO: I thought you never saw him.

BOITO: I didn't. Not that I remember. But I did see some of
the pictures. Christ! I don't want to be like that.
I've always wanted to be *original*.

FACCIO: Well, so have I. But look at me now — a conductor
of other men's music.

BOITO: It's not the same. You interpret. You *contribute*. My
job is to inspire, then make myself scarce. To be as
if I'd never been.

FACCIO: That's simply not true. Opera isn't songs without
words. People buy the libretti to read them.

BOITO: Only to see what's going on. They're about as interested in my *art* as a sailor is in the *art* of the chart-
maker. All he wants is not to run on the rocks. All
opera-goers want is not to make fools of themselves in the interval by getting the plot wrong.

FACCIO: Stop being so Polish!

BOITO: And now, with this damned new electric lighting, they're starting to turn off the house-lights during the performance, so no one can read the libretto anyway. It's chucked under the seat with the hats and umbrellas. The poet's labours languish in darkness, crushed beneath the well-cushioned bums of the music-lovers!

FACCIO: The composers still need you, Arrigo.

BOITO: Not much. Oh, God, if only Verdi had taken *Nero* off my hands! If only I didn't still imagine I might one day write music!

FACCIO: Of course you will.

BOITO: I won't.

FACCIO: You were writing last week.

BOITO: I threw it away. It was hopeless.

FACCIO: You're too self-critical.

BOITO: Well, I care about art. I've always cared about art. Nothing in the world is as important as art, it's the only way we can get a grip on *reality*, Franco. That's why — And that bloody old man, he doesn't give a toss! Not a toss!

FACCIO: Well, you have to remember the background. He's a peasant at heart.

BOITO: God, if he'd only had a proper education, what might he not have done!

FACCIO: Oh, written like Wagner, no doubt about it.

BOITO: But he's never understood the simplest things! The difference between form and formula, for instance. He just took over the formulae as he found them, pathetic, feeble, shallow — We've never had true operatic form in this country. It's all numbers — aria, rondo, cabaletta, stretta, ritornello, concertato — number one to number ten, twelve, sixteen, whatever — this bit, then that bit, then another bit — nothing composed *through*.

FACCIO: Like Wagner.

BOITO: Yes, of course, like Wagner! But better than Wagner! What we need is *music theatre*, everything composed as a whole, not a string of unrelated numbers! We should be using the vastest tonal and

rhythmical development! And we should be setting
great tragedies, not silly little libretti!

FACCIO: Ever thought of *Othello*?

BOITO: What?

FACCIO: [*rising*] I must go. Rehearsal.

BOITO: What do you mean, have I thought of *Othello*?

FACCIO: You said we ought to be setting great tragedies.

BOITO: I couldn't do *Othello*.

FACCIO: It's rather your subject — good and evil, darkness
          and light, angel and devil.

BOITO: I couldn't do it. I'm not a good enough musician.

FACCIO: I wasn't thinking of the music. Must go, Arrigo.
          Thanks for the drink.

BOITO: [*rising*] Here! What are you talking about? Franco!
          Come back here!

              [*But* FACCIO *has gone.*]

          Bloody hell! *Othello*!

              [*He goes and pours himself another drink.*]

          When Franco and I were young — which isn't
          nearly as long ago as it feels — we both knew
          exactly what was what. Franco wrote an opera
          called *The Flemish Fugitives*. It wasn't bad — they
          repeated it a few times at La Scala. But of course
          we thought he'd changed the entire course of
          musical history. We gave him a banquet. I wrote
          him an ode. 'To Italian Art', it was called. I've
          never regretted anything more in my life.

              [*He adopts a declamatory stance. Unknown to him,*
              VERDI *is listening.*]

          'Is this the man' — Faccio, you understand, aged
          23 —

          'Is this the man who shall restore
          Art to her altar, virginal and pure,
          Which now lies shattered, and her holy hall
          Obscenely spattered like a whorehouse wall!'

              [*He ends pointing accusingly at* VERDI.]

VERDI: Well, if I have indeed spattered the holy halls of
          art, why don't you get on and cleanse them? I'll be
          the first to come and light a candle at the pure new
          altar.

BOITO: [*appalled that* VERDI *has heard*] I didn't mean *me*! I
          meant —

VERDI: Yes, yes, the filth of the brothel, that's my life's
          work so far — *Nabucco, Ernani, Macbeth, Rigoletto* —
          obscenities each and every one!

BOITO: [*even more appalled*] I didn't mean — For heaven's
          sake! I meant —

VERDI: I'm really looking forward to hearing this 'music of
          the future'. It's very grand and sublime, I believe.
          So come on! Where is it? I want to see this altar, so
          foully defiled by swine like me, made pure and
          pristine by this glorious new music! Hallelujah for
          the Messiah of Italian art! What's your subject?

BOITO: [*mumble*] Mephistopheles.

VERDI: What?

BOITO: Mephistopheles.

VERDI: A peculiar choice for someone restoring chastity
          and purity, but come on — let's hear it!
          [BOITO *sings from his opera.*]

BOITO: [*singing*] 'I'm the spirit who denies you always, all
          the stars, the flowers' —

FACCIO: [*intervening*] Of course, it's much better in its
          revised form.

BOITO: [*singing*] 'I'm the force that never ceases, wrecks the
          rest of heaven on high' —

RICORDI: [*intervening*] It ran six hours, originally.

FACCIO: With interruptions.

VERDI: Interruptions?

FACCIO: From the audience.

BOITO: [*singing*] 'Chaos is my one desire.'

RICORDI: He'll never make a composer — I've never thought
          so. That's why I persuaded him to offer you *Nero*.

VERDI: That was kind of you and generous of him. Very
          generous.

BOITO: [*singing*] 'Ruin is my daily breath. And my life, and
          my hope, and my hope and living fire — universal
          wrack and death.'

VERDI: But he believes in the power of evil, in saying 'No'
          to the universe. Myself — I believe life is com-
          pletely pointless. But while we're in it, I much

prefer good to evil, and light to darkness. So — I
wrote my *Requiem*.

MEZZO: [*singing*] 'Lux aeterna luceat eis, Domine.'

BOITO: [*singing his reply*] 'I laugh! And I this little word let fly
— No!'

MEZZO: [*singing*] 'Cum sanctis tuis in aeternum quia pius
es' —

BOITO: [*singing*] 'Squeaking, shrieking, still I cry — No!
Biting, sneaking, struggling, shrieking, squeaking,
still I cry, with a hiss, with a hiss' —

[*His aria ends with derisive whistling.*]

VERDI: Well, if he will write the whistles and boos into his
own music —

[*The* TENOR *and* BASS/BARITONE *join the* MEZZO
for the remainder of the 'Lux aeterna'. BOITO *is
crushed. When the* SINGERS *finish we discover*
STREPPONI *alone.*]

STREPPONI: In the old days, I used to sit in a corner of his music
room as he composed. He'd try the phrases out on
me. He actually listened to what I said. He trusted
me. Pasticcio, I used to call him — my little pie. I
should have thought. Che pasticcio — What a
mess! [*serious*] In theory, of course, it's absolutely
right that a woman should devote herself exclusively to one man. In practice — and I say this very
reluctantly — it's probably a mistake. Because —
all questions of right and wrong aside — how many
men are really capable of devoting themselves
exclusively and for life to just one woman? Not that
he's a philanderer. No, that might have been
bearable. On the contrary, his nature is faithful,
loyal and loving. Which meant, when he fell in love
with Teresa, he had to give her all his love, all his
fidelity, all his loyalty. And to do that, he had to
take them away from me. And because he's a
decent man, a moral man, he knew he was doing
me wrong. And so the very sight of me drove him to
distraction. [*sad smile*] People talk such nonsense
about love. They're such hypocrites. They talk
about self-restraint and pulling oneself together,

when they know perfectly well what it's like. I
suppose they're afraid, and with reason. Verdi
could no more help himself falling in love than he
could help himself write music. Except that's when
he more or less stopped. He wasn't at peace with
himself, you see. He wasn't at peace with anyone.
He yelled at me, he screamed at the servants, he
was extremely unkind to old friends, he turned on
Ricordi — I tried to love her frankly and sincerely.
It seemed the only thing to do, but it only made
things worse. I treated her as my friend and had
her endlessly to stay. I wrote her very long letters,
which she didn't always answer. I was so insist-
ently, maddeningly nice to her, he could have
killed me. And I always behaved as though love
had never crossed either of their minds. I don't
think it did cross hers, as a matter of fact. No, I'm
fairly certain — as sure as one can be about these
things — that their intimacy was entirely musical.
She was a soprano, of course. She sang the *Requiem*
all across Europe. And as I listened, I thought time
would come to my rescue. It couldn't last. But it
did. I'd had him exclusively for twenty years. She
— how shall I put it? She absorbed him for ten. Ten
is far longer than twenty when you're not the one
he wants. Ten is eternal hell fire. By the end we
were living virtually *à trois*, and the papers were on
to it, and I could stand it no longer. It seemed to
me that fate had willed that my whole happiness in
life was lost. So I went to him and I said, 'Either
Teresa goes, or I go.' And he said — because it had
been hell for him, too — he said, 'Either she stays
or I blow my brains out.' [*tries to laugh*] All very
melodramatic! Suitably so, I suppose, for singers
and a composer. Though I myself always hated the
stage, even when I was on it — so much unreality
and delirium, and for what? But there we were, like
something out of an opera. And as I loved him, I
was the one who went away. Not far. Just to my
sister in Cremona.

    [*Pause.*]

Teresa didn't stay long. She went off to Russia to sing for six months, though officially she'd retired. She said it was the money, but — She never *loved* him, you see.

[*Pause.*]

I've come to religion very late But now I believe in the power of the man-god Jesus Christ to redeem us by his example. I have forgiven her her offences, and tried to love her. And time has done its work at last. We're friends again, Verdi and I. Love we do not speak of. I write his letters, I see he's not pestered by bores or strangers, I let him get on with the farming. If we'd had children, perhaps things would have been diferent. I'm not unhappy. But I am afraid. I'm afraid I've ruined his life. I'm afraid I stopped him writing. Which is why I'm grateful to Giulio. If we can get him writing again, I shan't feel I've — I'm — Of course, he won't ask me to sit in the corner again. But so long as he's writing — I have God. He has music.

[STREPPONI *goes to join* VERDI, RICORDI *and* FACCIO *who are sitting lingering over their wine after dinner.* VERDI *lights a cigar. He is feeling expansive.*]

VERDI: Of course, all this talk about the music of the future comes from people whose music, if any, lies *in* the future. When they come to write it, *if* they do, they'll find the future's disappeared. The moment they write the final chord, it's the music of the past. Mind you, they have all the time in the world to talk cant, composers, these days. One opera every five years, and they think they're over-worked. Forty and fifty years ago, now —

[STREPPONI *laughs at him. He's feeling contented enough to take it. The others are biding their time. But* FACCIO *is quite nervous.*]

No, but it's true. Galley-slaves we were. Whipped from opera to opera by desperate and dishonest impresarios, slamming down our notes like oars in the water.

STREPPONI: It could be fun, though, working under pressure.

VERDI: When one was young. But it was so exhausting! And we never had time to think what we were doing. No one respected the composer in those days. It was all the singers. They'd turn up — exhausted themselves, by the way — they sang up to six times a week —

FACCIO: Really?

STREPPONI: Oh, yes. And pregnant!

VERDI: They'd turn up at the opera house, take one look at your latest masterpiece and say, 'Oh, I can't possibly sing *that*.' Best aria in the opera, probably, but — 'No, no, it's too high, too low, too long, too short. I'll sing this, instead.' 'But, signora, that's by Rossini!' 'Is it? So what? It's very charming, it shows my voice off to perfection, and last time I did it here I was encored three times. So I shall sing it in Act Three instead of this absolutely impossible aria *you've* written.'

   [*Everyone laughs.*]

   You laugh, but it happened all the time. 'Suitcase-pieces' they were called.

RICORDI: Well, things *have* changed!

VERDI: Only because we fought for them. And *singers* haven't changed. From their point of view, all we do is provide notes. It's the voices the public comes to hear, not the music.

STREPPONI: You are a monster! It's not the voices the public wants, it's the drama.

VERDI: No, no — singers without songs — that's the singers' dream. Quite a good definition of modern opera, in my view.

   [FACCIO *can wait no longer and jumps in.*]

FACCIO: Like Rossini, you mean!

VERDI: [*astonished*] What?

FACCIO: [*aghast at his blunder*] Well, some of his operas — don't you think? — They have very empty — What you were saying —

VERDI: Rossini wrote some of the best music in all opera.

FACCIO: Yes, of course, but — there are passages in — in *Otello*, say — where —

STREPPONI: [*coming to the rescue*] I always loved singing Rossini.

Cinderella, The Thieving Magpie, Moses — I even sang
Desdemona once. Lovely willow song!

RICORDI: But a ludicrous opera.

[VERDI *looks at him sharply.*]

VERDI: Why do you say that? It has some very good stuff in
the last act.

RICORDI: Possibly. But the first two — absurd!

FACCIO: A travesty of Shakespeare.

STREPPONI: All about Roderigo!

RICORDI: As though we're interested in him! And the
greatest scene in the play simply left out!

VERDI: Iago, you mean. Iago tempting Othello into
jealousy.

RICORDI: Exactly!

FACCIO: You know your Shakespeare.

VERDI: I should hope so. The father of all modern drama.

RICORDI: Then you're rather a disloyal son, only to have set
Macbeth.

[VERDI *gives him a hard look.*]

VERDI: You know what happened when they first did
Rossini's *Otello* in Rome?

RICORDI: No?

VERDI: They gave it a happy ending.

RICORDI: Well, when someone's done as grotesque a botch
as that, I suppose it doesn't matter. Quite apart
from anything else, there are three tenors and no
baritone!

FACCIO: [*laughing*] Iago — the villain — a tenor!

STREPPONI: Well, don't blame Rossini. Those were the only
singers available at Naples that year, I expect.

RICORDI: I do blame him. I blame him very much, for ruining
one of the greatest tragedies in all drama.

VERDI: You should blame the librettist. What could
Rossini do with conventional trash like that?

RICORDI: He could refuse to set it.

FACCIO: [*still laughing*] Iago a tenor!

STREPPONI: I think you're dreadfully harsh. The last act really
does have lovely music.

VERDI: Ah, but there, my dear, the scenes are all properly
based on Shakespeare.

STREPPONI: Not the Gondolier's song!

VERDI: Borrowed from another great poet — Dante.

[*The* PIANIST *begins to play the introduction to the Gondolier's song.*]

So much depends on the quality of the libretto. People don't understand. You can't write an opera without *words*.

[*The* TENOR *sings 'Nessun maggior dolore' from Rossini's 'Otello'.* VERDI *speaks over the piano conclusion, thinking professionally.*]

Wonderful use of an off-stage voice, that, to set the mood for Desdemona's scene. 'There is no greater sorrow than to remember happiness in a time of great distress.' Wonderful words. Wonderful music.

FACCIO: Though how many gondoliers actually know their Dante —

[*He is quickly hushed.*]

STREPPONI: Poor Desdemona! Too innocent for her own good.

FACCIO: And Othello, the great man destroyed by one fatal flaw.

RICORDI: Jealousy — magnificent subject.

STREPPONI: The one emotion no one can control.

VERDI: Oh, but that's not the subject of *Othello*. The subject is power — the power of an evil man over a good one, to make him mad.

RICORDI: What the librettist left out, you mean.

VERDI: Yes, yes. Iago poisoning Othello's mind — that's the heart of it.

STREPPONI: Perhaps he left it out because it's too difficult to do.

VERDI: Nonsense! It's completely operatic! It cries out for music!

[*They all look at him. Pause.*]

Is this a conspiracy?

RICORDI: Maestro! How could you think such a thing? It just so happens that — that — well, I happen to know that someone's been planning a libretto of *Othello* and — and —

VERDI: Who?

[*Pause. Neither* RICORDI *nor* FACCIO *dare say.*]

STREPPONI: It's Boito.

[*Pause.*]

VERDI: I no longer compose. I've retired.

[*Pause*]

FACCIO: Won't you see him? Talk to him?

VERDI: There's no point. Nothing will come of it.

FACCIO: All the same —

[VERDI *shrugs.* RICORDI *and* FACCIO *go in pursuit of a highly reluctant* BOITO.]

BOITO: No! Really — please — I mean — I can't do it! I've only met him once in the last ten years, and that was in the waiting room at Bologna station. He talked about how difficult it is to sleep in sleeping cars. I ask you!

[*All his cockiness has gone. He is extremely nervous.*]

FACCIO: What did you say?

BOITO: I don't know. Some rubbish about how I don't sleep much anywhere, I expect. Look — Franco — my dear, old friend — I'm terribly sorry — I don't think I can face it.

FACCIO: Nonsense. Of course you can.

BOITO: I've got toothache. Agony. And terrible neuralgia — here. [*touches his jaw*] I think I'm getting an abscess.

RICORDI: Don't be ridiculous. Come on.

BOITO: I ought to go to the dentist — really. It'll be much less painful.

RICORDI: Do stop being so silly. He may be a bear, but he won't eat you. [*finding papers on the piano*] Is this the outline?

BOITO: [*terrified*] We're not taking it along!

FACCIO: Of course we are!

BOITO: But he may read it!

FACCIO: That's the whole idea, Arrigo. Pull yourself together. Where's your hat?

BOITO: [*blind with panic*] Hat — hat — hat — hat —

[*He can't see* RICORDI *holding it out for him. Huge relief.*]

You'll have to go without me. I can't find my hat.

[*Then he sees* RICORDI.]

Oh. Thanks.

RICORDI: Now gloves.

              [*Same business.*]

BOITO: Gloves — gloves — gloves — gloves — No gloves. Can't possibly call on Verdi without gloves.

              [*This time* FACCIO *is holding them out.* BOITO *gives him a nasty look.*]

Ah. My gloves. Thank you *so* much.

              [RICORDI *offers him a stick.*]

Better not take the stick. He might use it to beat me.

RICORDI: Ready?

BOITO: Of course not. I shall never be ready.

FACCIO: Let's go, then.

BOITO: [*completely sincere*] Franco, you do realise, I admire him more than any man on earth?

FACCIO: So do I. Come on.

              [BOITO *stays where he is.*]

BOITO: He's old enough to be my father.

RICORDI: And mine. So what?

BOITO: I've never had a father. How do you talk to them? What do you say? Are they human at all? Do they understand how sons *have* to rebel?

RICORDI: Of course. They were sons themselves once.

BOITO: But they forget. I bet they forget. Specially if they've never had sons of their own.

FACCIO: He had a son.

BOITO: [*astonished*] *Did* he?

FACCIO: A son and a daughter. They both died as children. So did the first wife.

BOITO: I knew there was a first wife, but —

RICORDI: Strepponi had children, too. Not his — before she met him. No one knows what became of them.

BOITO: [*overjoyed*] Strepponi? Illegitimate children?

RICORDI: Never mentioned, of course. Some tenor was the father, they *say*, but no one actually knows. Except Strepponi, presumably.

BOITO: Good God! Then they are both human after all!

FACCIO: Off we go, then.

BOITO: Oh, God! I feel like Ernani. In Verdi's opera. End of Act Two. Ernani going to meet Silva. Going to meet the challenge of his life!

[*The* TENOR *and the* BASS/BARITONE *begin to sing from the end of Act Two of 'Ernani', beginning with Silva's 'Now you come here and fight with me'. They continue as far as 'Will you give me your word?' Meanwhile* BOITO *has brought* VERDI *his outline, and* VERDI *reads it.* BOITO *gets more and more anxious. When the music ends, he can no longer contain himself.*]

I — I tried to simplify the story. I — he — I think the librettist has to do that, so the composer can develop the characters in the music. That's why I left out Act One.

VERDI: Yes.

BOITO: Shakespeare's Act One, I mean. I felt — unity of place is so important in this story. To convey the atmosphere — Cyprus — an island — somewhere they can't get off. Well, Desdemona can't get off.

VERDI: Quite.

BOITO: And we really don't need to know about her father and the elopement, do we? We want to get to the heart of the matter straight away — Othello, the victorious general, Iago plotting, and Desdemona — All the romantic wooing in Shakespeare's Act One, I've put that into the big duet.

VERDI: So I see. Yes. [*becomes almost too friendly*] I shall never forget your kindness, Boito, in offering me *Nero*. I'm sorry I was unable to take advantage of it. How are you getting on with it?

BOITO: [*flustered*] Well — I live immersed in the blood and perfume of Roman decadence, maestro, but somehow —

VERDI: You've been working on it some years now.

BOITO: Nine. Nine years.

FACCIO: Boito has many other commitments.

VERDI: Yes, indeed. You're too selfless. All these excellent libretti for other people when you're such a successful composer in your own right.

BOITO: Oh, well, I —

VERDI: Did I not read somewhere that you started on another classical subject?

BOITO: *Hero and Leander,* yes. But I — I abandoned it. I gave the libretto to Bottesini. His opera's being done next year.

VERDI: Bottesini! Your generosity knows no bounds. And then you've done several translations, I hear. From Russian *and* German. Wagner, for instance. You've translated a good deal of Wagner.

BOITO: [*dreading what's coming*] A little, yes.

VERDI: Oh, a good deal. He presents great difficulties, I imagine. German vowels are so different from our Italian ones.

BOITO: Yes, he's not easy, but —

VERDI: [*affable*] We last met, I think, after a performance of *Lohengrin.*

BOITO: Yes. Yes. At Bologna station. I went twice. To the opera, I mean, not the station.

VERDI: Really? Once was enough for me. Besides, people said my presence upset the musicians. I don't know what truth there was in that, but the orchestra certainly played abominably. They were vilely out of tune. And the production was dreadful.

BOITO: Oh, did you think so? I thought it was —

VERDI: The most appalling mess. But I've always admired the prelude. Fine — very fine. Wagner writes wonderfully for the orchestra. In the German manner, of course.

BOITO: Oh, wonderfully. I mean, some of the scoring in that prelude —

VERDI: And we should all be grateful to him for getting the conductor off the stage and into the orchestra pit. In the old days, you know, Faccio here would have stood facing the audience, his back to the singers, blocking everyone's view. Wagner stopped that.

BOITO: Thank goodness!

         [*It all seems to be going well, and* BOITO *is relaxing.*]

VERDI: Yes — yes. [*indicating the outline*] This is very good, you know.

BOITO: [*overjoyed*] Do you really think so?

VERDI: Very good indeed. [*then immediately withdrawing any personal commitment*] If I were you, I'd turn it into a

proper verse libretto. Someone may want it — you
never know.

BOITO: [*confused*] No. I mean, yes.

VERDI: Oh, and by the way. If I were you, I wouldn't
mention it to a soul. Not a soul. If it once got into
the papers — And you know what these journalists
are.

BOITO: Oh, yes! Quite!

VERDI: If I were you, I'd only ever refer to it by some code-
name.

BOITO: Code-name?

VERDI: Yes. Let me see — *Othello* — Why not — 'The
Chocolate Project'?

    [*He leaves the outline in* BOITO's *hands.*]
Goodbye!

    [*He has gone.* BOITO *is aghast and disgusted.*]

BOITO: 'The *Chocolate* Project'?

FACCIO: Well done!

BOITO: Did it go all right?

    [*No one is very sure.*]

FACCIO: Well — well, I *think* so.

BOITO: Then may I please go to the dentist? This tooth
really *hurts*.

    [RICORDI *is consulting* STREPPONI.]

RICORDI: What do *you* think?

STREPPONI: He was polite. That's something, I suppose.

RICORDI: Yes. I think he's interested.

FACCIO: So do I. I think.

BOITO: Please — dentist.

FACCIO: He didn't say he'd do it, though.

STREPPONI: Of course not. Really, Franco!

RICORDI: But he did tell Arrigo to put it into verse.

STREPPONI: Not specifically for him.

FACCIO: What did it mean, him not wanting Arrigo to talk
about it?

    [*For once* FACCIO *has got it right.*]

STREPPONI: Well, that *was* hopeful, I think.

RICORDI: Yes! He'd never say that if he wasn't really interested.

STREPPONI: Well —

RICORDI: I think he's hooked.

STREPPONI: I wouldn't say 'hooked', but —

RICORDI: Definitely, comprehensively hooked!

FACCIO: Well done, Arrigo!

BOITO: Oh, God! Now I really *am* Ernani. I've just handed over my horn to my dearest enemy. Handed over my life, in fact. All Verdi has to do now is blow my damned horn, and I'm his for ever.

> [*The* TENOR *and* BASS/BARITONE *pick up the scene from 'Ernani' again, with the* TENOR'*s 'Here's my promise'.* VERDI *comes to listen. He speaks over a piece of accompaniment.*]

VERDI: Early stuff. Aria, rondo, cabaletta, stretta, ritornello, concertato — number one to number ten. [*smile*] I don't write like that any more.

BOITO: [*very eager*] Any more? Then you do write?

> [VERDI *frowns angrily and turns away. The duet continues to the end of the Act, with* BOITO, RICORDI *and* FACCIO *singing as chorus.*]

[*Blackout.*]

END OF ACT ONE

ACT TWO

The PIANIST *plays the introduction to the Sleepwalking Scene from* VERDI's *'Macbeth' as the characters come on with candles. Soon a* DOCTOR *and a* GENTLEWOMAN *are talking urgently to music. Then* LADY MACBETH *appears with a lamp, and the scene continues to the end.*

When it is over, BOITO *comes on, applauding loudly.*

BOITO: There! Verdi inspired by Shakespeare! And written thirty years ago, before anyone had even *begun* to talk about music-drama. But that's what it is — not a number from an opera, a scene from a music-drama. He didn't want it *sung*, you know. He wanted it *acted*. He told the soprano — none of your lovely roulades rolling round the larynx — I want you *rough* — hollow — veiled — stifled — diabolic. [*sudden pain*] Ow! Christ – here comes Giulio!

　　　　[*He sits quickly at his desk, and pretends to be writing as* RICORDI *comes in.*]

RICORDI: Finished?

BOITO: [*muffled*] Not quite.

RICORDI: Where have you got to?

　　　　[*He takes the piece of paper that* BOITO *had been pretending to write on.*]

　　　　You lazy sod! You haven't written a word since last week!

BOITO: [*faint*] Toothache.

RICORDI: Nonsense! Get on and finish it!

BOITO: [*indignant*] Have you ever had an abscess in the mouth? It's like an enraged rhinoceros, charging at every nerve-end.

RICORDI: I thought it had burst.

BOITO: Not till yesterday. Besides, I'm depressed.

RICORDI: Oh, God! What now?

BOITO: I've been thinking about Piave.

RICORDI: What about him?

BOITO: What an appalling story! What an appalling poet!

RICORDI: He only happened to write *Ernani, Macbeth, Rigoletto, Traviata, Boccanegra* —

BOITO: Ten. He wrote *ten* libretti for the maestro, and
           never defended the choice of a single adjective. He
           was abused and reviled, and treated like a donkey.

RICORDI: I want to get *Boccanegra* back in the repertoire. It
           ought to be making us money. And it's full of good
           things.

BOITO: It's full of *bad* things, like everything he wrote.
           Before he had his stroke.

RICORDI: Yes. Poor Piave!

BOITO: Paralysed and out of his mind for eight years
           before he died. And his only claim to fame, the
           mystery that someone so utterly second-rate could
           inspire a genius.

RICORDI: Well?

BOITO: It's not much of a mantle to inherit, Giulio —
           minion to the maestro.

RICORDI: Now listen. You are a very much better poet than
           Piave.

BOITO: I'm not.

RICORDI: All right, you're not. But you've written an opera of
           your own, *and* you're writing another.

BOITO: I'm not.

RICORDI: [*fed up*] Look — do you want this mantle or not?

BOITO: Of course I do! I want the maestro to like me! I want
           him to think I'm quite all right, really, when you
           get to know me. I'm *not,* of course, but —

RICORDI: The maestro will never think better of you if you
           don't get on and finish *Othello*!

BOITO: Ssshh!

RICORDI: If you take much longer, the chocolate will go off
           the boil. And I shan't pay you.

BOITO: [*lofty*] If he doesn't like it, I shan't expect remuner-
           ation. This is a labour of love.

RICORDI: Well, get on and labour! If Desdemona's not stran-
           gled by tonight, I'll strangle you!

BOITO: I've been up since half-past seven, trying.
           Honestly.

RICORDI: Try harder. Get up at six.

BOITO: [*pathos*] You don't understand. My face aches like a
           fat soprano's corset.

RICORDI: What do you want? Laudanum?
        [BOITO *brightens at once.*]
BOITO: Oh, yes, please!
RICORDI: No. No drink or drugs till you've finished the libretto!
BOITO: You're a monster! A fiend!
        [*He beats the desk, as he once beat the keys of the piano.*]
RICORDI: Look — would it cure your toothache to go and talk things over with the maestro?
BOITO: [*pathos again*] I don't know. It might make me seize up altogether.
        [STREPPONI *joins* RICORDI.]
STREPPONI: Your friend seems very nervy.
RICORDI: Well — the artistic temperament, you know. A little oversensitive, perhaps.
STREPPONI: I was afraid so. Do try and keep him calm, Giulio. Verdi mustn't get the idea he's involved with someone — unbalanced. He doesn't care for nerves in other people.
RICORDI: They can't help having them.
STREPPONI: Of course not. I have them myself. But I never *show* them. Or he thinks I'm trying to put pressure on him. He hates any kind of pressure.
RICORDI: I see.
STREPPONI: So — keep Boito calm. Oh — and not a word to Verdi about this conversation, of course.
RICORDI: My lips are sealed. With chocolate.
STREPPONI: I'll see if I can persuade him to let you pay a visit.
        [*She goes to* VERDI, *but he is already up.*]
VERDI: No!
STREPPONI: Why not?
VERDI: I should feel committed.
STREPPONI: Just having them here for a couple of days' discussions?
VERDI: Of course. I'd have to read what he's written.
STREPPONI: You might like it.
VERDI: Then I'd have to say so. Which would commit me at once.
STREPPONI: Couldn't you like it, but not want to do it?

VERDI: [*ignoring her*] Then I might like *parts* of it. Which
              would be even worse. I should feel obliged to
              suggest amendments, and he would feel obliged to
              make them, and I'd be even more committed
              because he'd have done them for me.

STREPPONI: Oh, well, let's just hope you hate the whole thing!
              Then we can forget the entire business!

VERDI: Really, Peppina, you're being very stupid about
              this. If I dislike it I shall want to say so. But how
              can I? To his face? In my own house?

STREPPONI: You don't always hold your tongue at home.
                          [*Her tone is neutral, but* VERDI *doesn't like it.*]

VERDI: Anyone would think you *wanted* them here.

STREPPONI: It would be company. I like Giulio.

VERDI: Giulio's not the point! Though he is. He's quite
              clearly asked to come here to embarrass me. To try
              and force me into *Otello.* Well, in your reply, kindly
              make it quite clear that I do not at all appreciate
              this kind of pressure. Tell him, far and away the
              best thing is for Boito to finish the libretto —
                          [BOITO *groans and buries his head in his hands.*]
              — then send it to me here, where I can read it at
              leisure, without committing myself in any way till
              I've made up my mind. When I've done *that* — then
              Giulio can bring him. [*sarcastic*] *If* he still wants to.
              Tell him all that. And let me see the letter before it
              goes.
                          [*Lights dim on* STREPPONI *and* VERDI, *and rise on*
                          BOITO *and* RICORDI *again.*]

RICORDI: Obviously very excited.

BOITO: Hmm!

RICORDI: Simply can't wait to see the finished thing. So —
              get on and finish it!
                          [*He shoves* BOITO *down into a chair and comes to
                          address the audience.*]
              God, what *nonsense!* All this subterfuge and silliness!
              Children — that's what they are, the whole
              damned lot of them. As it happens, I like children,
              fortunately for them. Because they troop through
              my office — composers, conductors, singers,
              musicians, librettists — like refugees from life,

demanding the most expensive toys. But it's not really jewels they want, or fur coats, or houses crammed with vulgar furniture. No. They want love. I mean, look at Boito. An intelligent man — really very intelligent. But — no proper girl-friend, no wife, no family, no proper country, even. An orphan abandoned to Art. And who does he come to for comfort? Me. And Verdi — he has got Strepponi, it's true, but the man's so obviously bored and unhappy, it leaks from every pore. When I go to see him, I wear galoshes. He's proud, obstinate, wilful — afraid. They're all afraid all the time. Of each other to start with. Of the critics. Of their lovers or livers or both. Even of me, thank God. The tantrums, the passions, the rages, the jealousies — it's all fear. Fear they'll lose 'it', whatever 'it' may be. They're terrified that normal, everyday life, with normal everyday pains and pleasures would ruin 'it' for ever. Genius can't exist without neurosis — what twaddle! But with them, it's an article of faith. So whatever you do, don't be normal, don't be happy, feel ill at *least* twenty-four hours a day. Christ! Do I *really* like children? They drive me bankrupt, they drive me mad. What about me, I want to scream at them. Where am I supposed to find all this love you insist on?

[*He turns angrily on* BOITO]

For Christ's sake, how much longer are you going to be?

[BOITO *smiles and hands the libretto to him, like a child offering teacher an apple.*]

BOITO: Finished!

RICORDI: Well done!

[*He gives the libretto straight to* VERDI.]

What do you think?

VERDI: It needs work.

[BOITO *groans.*]

Act Three. It needs a better curtain.

[BOITO *groans again.*]

But it's on the right lines. I'll buy it.

RICORDI: He loves it! He *loves* it!

                    [*He begins to dance triumphantly round* VERDI.]
VERDI: Put it in the file with *King Lear*, would you?
                    [RICORDI *stops dancing. He takes the libretto from*
                    VERDI.]
         I may want to look at it again one day. Thank him
         for me, won't you?
                    [*The* PIANIST *plays the 'Requiem' theme.*]
BOITO: Well, that's it, isn't it? I mean, that's — I mean —
         Oh, Christ!
RICORDI: Now don't be silly.
BOITO: He's simply not interested. Never was! Oh, well —
         What does it matter? Only another six months of
         my life gone down the drain —
RICORDI: Look, he's *bought* it.
BOITO: Oh, well, he can afford to, can't he?
RICORDI: All he wants is a new end to Act Three.
                    [*But* BOITO *is huffy now.*]
BOITO: Oh, yes, a nice old-fashioned concertato! Everyone
         standing about emoting in suspended time! A
         number! Well, he's not getting that from *me*!
RICORDI: He didn't say that. He said he wanted a better
         curtain.
BOITO: How *can* he have a better curtain? Good God,
         Othello's mad with jealousy, he's just slapped
         Desdemona's face in front of the representative of
         the Doge of Venice, he's gone completely out of
         control in front of most of the population of
         Cyprus, Iago's triumphant, Desdemona's in tears
         — what more does he want?
RICORDI: [*careful*] Well, I rather gather he'd like to bring back
         the Turks.
BOITO: The Turks? But I drowned every last Turk before
         the opera began, in the storm!
RICORDI: Ah. They weren't drowned, it seems, merely dis-
         persed. Now they've all got together again —
         drums, trumpets, canons firing — they're on the
         attack.
BOITO: How ridiculous!
RICORDI: Othello shakes himself like a lion, straightens up,
         unsheathes his sword and says, 'Everyone follow
         me! Once again Othello leads the Venetians to

                victory!'
BOITO: He can't say that! 'Everyone follow me!' He can't
            possibly! He's frantic, out of his mind with misery
            and jealousy! My God, if Verdi had written his own
            librettos like Wagner, he'd never have got
            anywhere! How can Othello just pull himself
            together and say 'Everyone follow me', as though
            nothing has happened?
RICORDI: That could be a difficulty, I do see —
BOITO: A man who can pull himself together doesn't go off
            and defeat the Turks, then come back and pick up
            where he left off, going mad again and killing his
            wife. That's just preposterous.
RICORDI: Ah, but if Desdemona's left alone on stage, except
            for weeping attendants, and prays for Othello's
            success in spite of the way he's treated her — It
            does make a damned good curtain.
BOITO: But how does he expect me to make sense of it
            psychologically?
RICORDI: You're the writer.
                [*Pause.*]
BOITO: Oh, God! I swore to myself I'd stand up to him,
            that I wouldn't be Piave!
RICORDI: Look, no one's asking you to go against your
            artistic conscience.
BOITO: No?
RICORDI: Try it his way, that's all. If it works, it works. If it
            doesn't, think up a better ending yourself. What
            does Shakespeare do at that point?
BOITO: Shakespeare? Oh, he has Othello going off saying,
            'Goats and monkeys'.
RICORDI: That won't do.
BOITO: No. No — I suppose it might just be plausible if —
            It could show the greatness of Othello's character.
RICORDI: What?
BOITO: If — in the midst of his terrible personal catas-
            trophe, he was able to remember his patriotic duty.
RICORDI: Oh, Verdi's always been fond of the calls of duty.
BOITO: While the inner man crumbles, the outer goes on
            like a good public servant.
RICORDI: That's the idea!

BOITO: It's not an *idea*. It's a desperate remedy.

RICORDI: Give it a try, though, won't you? I promised him you would.

BOITO: Well —

RICORDI: My dear old friend, don't make me look a fool! Do it for me.

BOITO: If I do it for anyone, I'll do it for me!

[RICORDI *puts his arm around* BOITO's *shoulder.*]

RICORDI: I knew you would! By the way, Verdi's let it be known he thinks La Scala should do your *Mephistopheles*. What do you think?

BOITO: [*thrilled*] La Scala! Everyone follow me!

[*They go,* RICORDI's *arm firmly guiding* BOITO. *As they go, they meet* VERDI, *who takes the new scene from* BOITO *and at once questions him.*]

VERDI: And now — what do *you* think of it?

BOITO: [*alarmed*] Me?

VERDI: You didn't want to write this scene, I know. But you've done it. Now I want to know if you believe in it.

[BOITO *takes a deep breath.*]

BOITO: No, maestro.

VERDI: Why not?

BOITO: Because it breaks the logic of the tragedy. Shakespeare spends three acts building up a more and more stifling atmosphere. Othello and Desdemona are like two people trapped in an airless room, slowly asphyxiating. If one of them can suddenly pull himself together and walk out of the room to fight the Turks — well — it's like a fist smashing through the window, letting in air. The characters come to. Iago's spell is broken. The tragedy can't happen. And to re-establish that atmosphere would take another three acts.

VERDI: I see. Yes. But —

BOITO: It would take a *dramatist* another three acts. But — Music is infinitely more potent a medium than language. A few bars — and perhaps you have something in mind already, maestro — a few bars from you, and perhaps the problem *can* be solved.

Perhaps the atmosphere can be re-established and
the tragedy go on.

VERDI: [*genuine admiration*] What a wonderfully clear mind
you've got, Boito!

BOITO: *Have* you a musical solution, maestro?

VERDI: I wish I had. But to tell you the truth — [*ironical*] I
don't believe even *I* could produce one. Even
music has its limitations, you know.

> [*He moves away. Everyone looks accusingly at*
> BOITO.]

FACCIO: Well, what do we do now?

STREPPONI: We must think up a better curtain for the act.

RICORDI: Better curtain for the act, Franco.

FACCIO: Yes.

RICORDI: We need a better curtain for the act.

FACCIO: I know.

RICORDI: Well, think of one!

> [*Silence. Then* BOITO *comes up with the solution.*]

BOITO: I shall alter Shakespeare!

RICORDI: Are you sure that's wise?

BOITO: The order of events. You know the scene where
Othello is so overcome with emotion that he faints
away —

STREPPONI: You can't change that.

BOITO: No. In Shakespeare that comes *before* the arrival
of Lodovico. But if we put it after —

FACCIO: How? I don't see where.

BOITO: After the grand concertato. Iago should carry the
drama forward, tricking and teasing Othello till he
can't stand it any longer, and drives everyone out
of the room, cursing Desdemona, causing general
consternation, and —

STREPPONI: Will there be something for the chorus? He does
like to use the chorus.

RICORDI: Actually, I was hoping he might do this without a
chorus at all.

BOITO: No! Yes! All this is happening on the day of the
victory parade. Offstage, the crowd is coming to
proclaim Othello's triumph.

FACCIO: Ah! Very good!

BOITO: And Othello, alone with Iago, can stand the strain
         no longer. He faints. And Iago triumphs over his
         prostrate body, while the crowd calls for Othello
         from the square outside.
                 [*He is very pleased with his idea. The others aren't
                 sure.*]
         Of course, I've only sketched it out in my head so
         far, but —
VERDI: The trouble is, I've no time.
                 [*They all turn and look at him.*]
BOITO: What?
VERDI: No time for *Otello*. It's so long since I wrote an
         opera. It's a daunting prospect at my age. I feel I
         need to limber up on something else. It's Giulio's
         idea, really.
RICORDI: I've asked him to have another go at *Boccanegra*.
BOITO: [*seeing what's coming*] Oh, you have, have you?
VERDI: You will give me a hand, won't you?
RICORDI: Piave's libretto's so feeble in places.
BOITO: Poor Piave!
RICORDI: It won't be a major revision.
VERDI: Won't you?
RICORDI: It won't take long.
                 [*It's the last thing* BOITO *wants. But he has no
                 choice.*]
BOITO: Not a major revision! It'll take *months*! The plot —
         Piave's plot! No one's ever understood it — not
         even Piave. It's all about fourteenth-century
         politics in Genoa, for God's sake! But the music —
         the music's stood up pretty well.
                 [*The* PIANIST *has begun the music for Gabriele's
                 aria.*]
         [*sings*] 'Amelia!' [*speaks*] Twenty-five years old, this
         is. [*sings*] 'Amelia!' [*speaks*] Not bad at all. [*sings*]
         'Oh, God in heaven, have pity, my heart is torn in
         two.' [*speaks*] Very nice, very tuneful.
                 [*He sings the aria 'Kind heaven restore my love to
                 me'.*]
         Well, there you are! Very old-fashioned, of course.
         A cadenza at the end and all! But nice, very, very
         nice. As for the opera — I've done what I can. I've
         added quite a big new scene — half an act, really.

Based on Petrarch. Always go to the top when you steal a scene.

[*He goes to join* VERDI, *who is gazing out at the audience.* STREPPONI *is there.*]

VERDI: How much do you think they understand of what we're doing?

BOITO: Oh, almost nothing. But it doesn't matter with singers.

VERDI: I meant the audience.

BOITO: Oh! Well —

VERDI: I love the audience. *Wagner* likes them to sit in ecstatic silence. But what I like is when the whole theatre is carried away by a single emotion, when the audience truly· participates in the action, trembling, quivering, weeping —

BOITO: I've — I've never had that experience with my own one opera.

STREPPONI: Oh, but I hear you triumphed at La Scala.

BOITO: With the critics, yes. We went off like a firework — great whizzings and bangings.

VERDI: Oh, I *am* pleased. [*And he is.*]

BOITO: Unfortunately we went on like a firework. We petered out with pathetic little crackles.

STREPPONI: I don't understand.

BOITO: No one came.

VERDI: Why ever not?

BOITO: There was an overwhelming rival attraction. The circus. Star-spangled ladies on piebald ponies. *They* were *immensely* popular.

STREPPONI: Oh, my dear Boito, I *am* sorry.

BOITO: Oh, no need to be. I'm happy enough to be critically successful. I was a critic once, you see.

VERDI: I remember.

BOITO: Yes, for a man with only one opera I'm really getting to see Europe. It's Naples next.

VERDI: Oh, you'll do very well in Naples, I'm sure.

[BOITO *moves away. As he does so,* RICORDI *and* FACCIO *bring a newspaper over to* STREPPONI.]

RICORDI: Have you seen this interview Boito gave in Naples?

[BOITO *interviews himself, taking a glass of wine from the piano.*]

BOITO: [*interviewer*] Signor Boyto — [*himself*] Bo-*ito*,
          actually. [*interviewer*] Oh. Signor Botio, it seems a
          bit strange, a composer as successful as yourself,
          writing so many libretti for other people. [*himself*]
          Oh, I don't know. If one has the knack — [*inter-
          viewer*] Wouldn't you rather be writing the music of
          Otello yourself? [*himself, very expansive*] Good Lord,
          no! No, as a matter of fact, I'd always thought the
          whole subject far too tragic for opera. [*interviewer*]
          That's very interesting. Would you like to say why?
          [*himself, the authority on dramatic form*] Well, opera is a
          lyric form, you see, and *Othello* is so much a
          dramatic *tragedy*, I thought the one could never
          contain the other. But once I started working with
          Verdi — well — the maestro, you know! [*interviewer*]
          All the more reason, surely, to want to write the
          music yourself? [*himself*] Well, *want* to — yes, of
          course. There's nothing I'd like more. [*interviewer*]
          Well, why don't you, then? [*himself, meaning he never
          would have the talent*] I'd love to be able to!

STREPPONI: I'm sure he didn't mean that.

BOITO: But I regret very much that I can't.

STREPPONI: He probably didn't even say it. You know what
          journalists are.

VERDI: It's down here in black and white! Look! [*reading it in
          the opposite sense to* BOITO'*s meaning*] 'I'd love to be able
          to write the music myself.' We must get this
          cleared up at once. I'd come to like and trust that
          man.

STREPPONI: I'm sure it's just a misunderstanding.

VERDI: It's not that he wants to write the music himself —
          I can understand that. But he obviously thinks I'll
          never be able to do it to his satisfaction.

STREPPONI: How on earth do you read that into it?

VERDI: 'I regret very much that I can't write it *myself*.' And
          he's right to regret it. I shall never be able to please
          him.

          [FACCIO *and* RICORDI *have chosen this moment to
          remind* VERDI *to get on with 'Otello', by presenting
          him with a chocolate cake with 'Otello' on it.*]
          What the hell is that?

RICORDI: ⎫
FACCIO: ⎭ Good luck with 'The Chocolate Project'!

VERDI: For Christ's sake!

> [*With a furious gesture, he waves the cake away and turns angrily back to* STREPPONI.]

No, no. I shall have to give him the libretto back.

STREPPONI: But you've started setting it.

VERDI: It doesn't matter. Tell him there's no resentment, no bitterness. I quite understand. And he can have it for nothing, though I paid him for it. He can have it as a gift.

STREPPONI: [*who has had enough*] All right, then — I will give it back! Then we can have done with the whole business.

> [VERDI *is not expecting this.*]

Yes, you go back to bullying the peasants. It'll make a change from bullying me.

> [*He is even more taken aback.*]

All these excuses — they don't deceive anyone. They certainly don't deceive me. And if everyone else is too frightened to tell you, I'm not. I know you, I know you inside out. You've lost your nerve. That's all it is. You're *afraid* to write *Otello*. And if you really think you can't do it, say so. I've had enough. [*change of tone*] You know, and I know, you're longing to write it. For heaven's sake, for your own sake — give yourself this one last chance to be — Stop blaming everyone else. Just get on and *do* it.

> [BOITO *has come quietly to join them.*]

BOITO: Maestro, I only wrote this libretto for the honour of having you set it. To have my name linked to yours and Shakespeare's. To see you pick up the pen and start writing again. It's all yours — theme, libretto, opera. If it works — the libretto, I mean — it's because I've done it for *you*, seen the tragedy through *your* eyes, accommodated it to *your* genius.

VERDI: Oh, it works — *it* works very well.

BOITO: I don't know if you know what my life's like. I've been working on *Nero* for nine years now. Well — working! On the days I do work, I spend my whole

VERDI: time telling myself what an incompetent ass I am.
The days I don't, I tell myself: I'm a lazy sod.
Excuse me, signora. But so my life runs away.
Because I've chosen a subject, probably far beyond
my powers, but which totally obsesses me.

VERDI: [*touched at last*] You really should get on and finish
it, you know.

BOITO: Oh, it doesn't much matter whether I do or not.

VERDI: [*not to be outdone in bids for sympathy*] Of course, *I* may
not finish *Otello.*

BOITO: Oh, for pity's sake, don't abandon it now! You were
born to write it! And I know you've begun. [*to*
STREPPONI] He has begun, hasn't he? [*very anxious*]
Hasn't he?

VERDI: [*fretful*] There's been too much talk about it.

STREPPONI: He's done most of the first act.

BOITO: Wonderful!

VERDI: I'm too old. [*unhappy*] I've written so much. [*then the
confession of his real fear*] I couldn't bear people to say
I've written one opera too many.
[*Pause.*]

BOITO: Can I help at all?

VERDI: I don't think so, really. Thank you.

BOITO: Because — I do know my limitations, you know. I
do know my own unaided work's no good.

STREPPONI: Nonsense.

BOITO: It doesn't matter. It's not important. But though I
can't write for myself, I can write for you. So — if
there's something you want me to alter —

VERDI: You're very kind, but —

BOITO: Oh, it's not kindness. It's sheer egotism. I want to
bask in your glory.

VERDI: Well, if there is any glory, you shall certainly bask
in it. But it's not your talent I doubt. It's my own.
[*Pause.*]

BOITO: [*hesitant*] I have been thinking — You know we were
talking about Iago — his character and so on.

VERDI: Yes?
[RICORDI *and* FACCIO *now join in.*]

RICORDI: Most important person in the opera.

[VERDI *and* BOITO *look at him.*]

VERDI: Yes, well — there would be no drama without him, certainly.

BOITO: You know, it's never been clear why Iago sets out to destroy Othello.

FACCIO: Oh, he's the personification of evil, surely.

BOITO: Yes, but he's not Mephistopheles, you know — no horn and tail.

FACCIO: No, but the audience must be able to recognise him as the villain.

VERDI: He mustn't be played as a demon. He mustn't be warped and ugly.

BOITO: No. He should be positively handsome, in fact.

FACCIO: Really? Oh, I hadn't —

VERDI: I see him as tall, thin — thin lips, and eyes set close together — face like a priest. He's almost indifferent to what he says and does.

BOITO: Completely nonchalant.

VERDI: Says the most evil things in the most ordinary tone of voice.

BOITO: If someone's shocked, he just shrugs and says, 'Really? Do you think so? How's your wife?'

VERDI: He's as cool and indifferent to things as that — as *apparently* indifferent.

BOITO: You know, I think he should have a solo — a credo — something expressing his philosophy of life.

RICORDI: Like your Mephistopheles.

BOITO: A little, but —

FACCIO: There's nothing like that in Shakespeare.

VERDI: *This* is an *opera*.

BOITO: It's only an idea, but —

[*The* PIANIST *begins the introduction to Iago's Credo.*]

Hm. Hm. Very powerful. [*He means the music.*]

[*The* BASS/BARITONE *begins the Credo.*]

VERDI: [*to* FACCIO, *half-way through Iago's introduction*] And very Shakespearean.

[*At the end* VERDI *is very excited.*]

Marvellous! You've solved it! Now I know how to do Iago! The temptation scene! Iago — Otello —

[*The* TENOR *joins the* BASS/BARITONE *for the scene from Act Two of the opera, beginning 'How disturbing' ('Ciò m'accora'). At the end,* VERDI *is delighted.*]

Now we can say — Otello is!

[*Everyone relaxes as* VERDI *starts to hold forth.*]

Now it's very important in this music-*drama*, that the drama is as important as the music. The acting is as important as the singing.

[*Heads nod: they've heard it all before.*]

I want the greatest possible naturalism. I don't want *operatic* acting. I *hate* operatic acting. I want nature, not art.

[*Nod, nod.*]

But you must be careful not to concentrate so much on the acting that the singing goes by the board.

[*Nod, nod.*]

We must always *hear* you. Of course, before the first rehearsal, Faccio will have taken you all through your parts. Faccio! Where's Faccio?

BOITO: Faccio!

[FACCIO *seems to have disappeared. Now he pops up again.*]

FACCIO: Faccio's rehearsing. He's always rehearsing. Not just the singers, though God knows that takes long enough. You have to teach them the music, note by note, and the character *in* the music, and you have to stop the young tenor seizing on every high note like a terrier seizing a rat, and the ageing soprano ducking and weaving towards *her* high notes, like a drunk approaching a lamp-post. And then there's the orchestra, most of whom lost all interest years ago, and weren't very good then. The brass can't wait to get to the bar, the strings have sentimental attachments, the percussion read dirty books behind the bass drum. They all think they've heard it all before. If the conductor's a necessary evil, the emphasis is all on the evil. And it's not just one orchestra I have to think of. We're doing *Otello* in Venice after this, and that means rescoring all the

horn parts to trumpets — the Venetian horns
sound as though they're playing under water. For
Naples, I'll have to rewrite violas for second
violins. I tell you, I'm up till two every morning.
And whatever I do, the singers complain. Every
orchestra in the world is too loud for the singers.
And the composer's told me time and again — am I
going deaf or something? — when he writes dotted
crotchets, he means *dotted,* and I'm taking the
whole of Act Two too slowly. As for the public, I'm
that rude man with his back to the audience, who
only turns round to claim the applause they *meant*
for the singers and orchestra. It's insane! Why be a
conductor? Because you never get it right. You see
— There's music out here, music we make, music
we hear. And there's music in here. [*taps his head*]
Real music. Music no one ever quite hears. I know
what *Otello* should sound like, I know better than
Verdi. But there's always something imperfect — a
singer, a player, me — even, dare I say it? — a
misjudgement by the master. So I go on standing
out there, night after night, with a rod in my hand,
casting and casting my fly out over the pit,
catching the odd big fish, but never the fish in my
head, never perfection. But always hoping that —
well, that one night, he'll catch me.

BOITO: Faccio! Oh, Franco, *there* you are. He says all the
sopranos are hopeless. They're either too fat or
inaudible or both.

FACCIO: I did warn you.

BOITO: We must find someone else. Quickly.

FACCIO: The only soprano who can do Desdemona is Panta-
leone.

BOITO: But you're engaged to her.

FACCIO: So what?

BOITO: Verdi thinks you're trying to push her because
you're in love with her.

FACCIO: Has he heard her?

BOITO: No, but —

FACCIO: Well, come on! At least let's audition her.

[*At the appropriate moment the* PIANIST *starts the introduction to the scene where* DESDEMONA *comes to ask* OTHELLO *for Cassio's pardon.*]

BOITO: Has she the range?

FACCIO: Yes.

BOITO: I don't mean vocally, I mean emotionally.

FACCIO: She's the most emotional woman I've ever met.

BOITO: God, and you *still* want to marry her?

FACCIO: She has a wonderful innocence, Arrigo.

BOITO: That's all very well, but can she be subtle?

FACCIO: Oh, yes.

BOITO: Passionate?

FACCIO: Very.

BOITO: All three at once? That's what she's got to be in the scene where she comes to plead for Cassio's pardon.

FACCIO: Just listen.

[OTHELLO *and* DESDEMONA *begin the duet, and continue to the point where it is about to develop into the quartet.* VERDI *has been listening. At this point he stops them.*]

VERDI: Yes, yes, very good, charming, charming, stop there, would you?

[*He comes to the* SOPRANO.]

Not bad, not bad at all, but — When you're embracing Othello, remember you *love* him. You were being much too restrained there, much too cool. No wonder he had his suspicions. This is how you should do it. [*embracing her*] You love him physically. You can't have enough of his *body*. You —

FACCIO: [*intervening hastily*] I think perhaps a breather for the singers now, maestro.

VERDI: What? But we've only just begun! No, no, no — come on. Back to 'If unknowing, I've done wrong, husband forgive me', then on into the quartet. Iago! Emilia!

[*The* SINGERS *take up the music and continue to the end of the quartet.*]

Good! Very good! Thank you. Break there. [*to* BOITO] Not bad. I'll have her to stay for a few weeks. Teach her how to do it.

BOITO: Franco won't like that.

VERDI: Franco can concentrate on Emilia. She needs a lot of work. Now — the libretto.

BOITO: Not more changes!

VERDI: No, no — the printing. For the programme. Giulio — I'm most anxious that it's properly laid out, so people can read all the verses of the grand concertato in columns across the page. They must know what's going on. I don't want them turning back and forth to see where they are. Will you see it's done properly?

RICORDI: Of course.

VERDI: It's so important that people *understand*. I can't comprehend the Germans, sitting in the dark without a libretto to follow the story. Absurd! Now — Faccio — do you think they've got their breaths back yet?

FACCIO: Well —

VERDI: Good! On! The end of the play!

[*The* TENOR *and* SOPRANO *begin the final scene of 'Otello' from 'Who's there?' to the end, when they are joined by the* MEZZO *and the* BASS/BARITONE. *At the end* BOITO, FACCIO, STREPPONI *and* RICORDI *come to congratulate the* SINGERS, *but* VERDI *stays at the piano.*]

Awful now it's over, isn't it? I shall be so lonely. Every morning I've woken to love, anger, jealousy, deceit — all the emotions of our characters. And I've said to myself — Hurray! This scene to do today! And how the hell am I going to do that bit? And even after I'd finished the writing, there were the casting, the rehearsals, the problems, the doubts, the struggle to get those damned singers to *act*. I came home so excited every evening. I love the theatre. It's a glorious life. I haven't felt tired once. But now — it's over.

[*The rest of the cast look at him.*]

RICORDI: Is it? [*Pause.*] You've never really written a comedy, have you, maestro?

[*They begin to gather round him.*]

STREPPONI: And of course Shakespeare was a great *comic* writer, as well as a tragedian.

VERDI: Please!

BOITO: Funny you should say that. I was looking at *The Merry Wives of Windsor* only this afternoon. Had to do something, waiting for the first night.

VERDI: But I'm seventy-four!

FACCIO: Just about Falstaff's age, the way I see him.

BOITO: I've one or two ideas — I don't know if you're busy, maestro?

[*The* PIANIST *starts the opening bars of* VERDI's *'Falstaff'.*]

VERDI: Falstaff!

[*Everyone begins to flee.*]

Falstaff!

[*He drives everyone from the stage. He pulls out a pistol as the* PIANIST *strikes the last chord and prepares to shoot him —*]

[*Blackout.*]

THE END

Also available from Amber Lane Press:

Julian Mitchell   ANOTHER COUNTRY

One of the West End's resounding successes of 1982, winning the SWET award for 'Play of the Year'. The setting is an English public school in the 1930's. The two central characters, Guy Bennett and Tommy Judd, are both, in their own different ways, rebels and outsiders who dare to fight against the system.

Julian Mitchell   FRANCIS

Francis of Assisi was a man totally dedicated to a missionary life of poverty and simplicity. He wished to follow the gospels literally and to be a true disciple of Christ. In this play Julian Mitchell writes about the forces that turned Brother Francis into Saint Francis.

Ronald Harwood   THE DRESSER

Michael Billington found *The Dresser* '...a wonderfully affectionate and intelligent play about the theatre. It captures not only the equivocal relationship between star and dresser, it also conveys the bitchiness, the sentiment, the anecdotage, plus the feeling that the backstage world is itself a little kingdom, a tatty Camelot worshipping a prop Holy Grail.' Released as a feature film in 1984, starring Albert Finney and Tom Courtenay.

Ronald Harwood   TRAMWAY ROAD

Set in Cape Town in 1951, one year after the Population Registration Act was passed in South Africa. In the 1950s Tramway Road was a notorious Cape Coloured ghetto located within the predominantly white residential suburb of Sea Point. Ronald Harwood explores the influence that Tramway Road exerts over four characters: an expatriate English couple, Arthur and Dora Langley; Emil, a young man with dreams of becoming an actor in London; and Jacob, a house servant.

Brian Clark   WHOSE LIFE IS IT ANYWAY?

The play that launched Brian Clark to fame in 1978 when it transferred from the Mermaid to the Savoy Theatre en route for smash-hit success on Broadway. The central character is faced with a future of total dependence on a life-support machine. In his fight to determine the course of his own life – and death – he encounters fierce opposition from the medical profession.

Brian Clark   CAN YOU HEAR ME AT THE BACK?

Brian Clark's second West-End stage play, where he turns his attention to the world of architects and town planners who, instead of designing buildings that fit the human scale, seem only to succeed in creating a succession of 'people filing cabinets'.

Brian Thompson   TURNING OVER

A deliciously funny satire on how television documentaries are made. A BBC film crew is on a hill station in India, making a programme for a series entitled 'I could be happy here'. But the presenter, director and technicians are far from happy as they battle with the climate, the food and the souring relationships.

Hugh Whitemore   PACK OF LIES

Based on the real events surrounding an American couple living in Britain, Helen and Peter Kroger, who were found guilty of spying for the Russians in 1961. The action centres around the Jackson family who as friends and neighbours of the Krogers are drawn into a conspiracy of betrayal.

For a complete catalogue of our plays write or telephone:
Amber Lane Press, 9 Middle Way, Oxford OX2 7LH.
Tel. Oxford 50545